Slaves to Soldiers

Slaves to Soldiers

African-American Fighting Men in the Civil War

by Wallace B. Black

A First Book

Franklin Watts

A Division of Grolier Publishing
New York - London - Hong Kong - Sydney
Danbury, Connecticut

Photos ©: Archive Photos: 19, 29; The Boston Athenaeum: 34; Corbis-Bettmann: cover, 6, 14, 17, 21, 38, 47; Culver Pictures: 53; Illustrated London News: 10; Library of Congress: 16, 27, 41, 48, 49; Miles Educational Film Production/John W. Ravage: 8; The New-York Historical Society: 28; North Wind Picture Archives: 42; Official Department of Defense photograph: 44 (Helene C. Stikkel); Stock Montage, Inc.: 36; U.S. Military Academy, West Point, McGraighead Collection: 51; UPI/Corbis-Bettmann: 9, 24. All other photographs are public domain.

Visit Franklin Watts on the Internet at:
http://publishing.grolier.com

Library of Congress Cataloging-in-Publication Data

Black, Wallace B.
Slaves to soldiers: African-American fighting men in the Civil War / by Wallace B.
    Black
p.   cm.—(A first book)
Includes bibliographical references (p. 60) and index.
Summary: Explores the circumstances of African-Americans who fought in the Civil
    War, including slaves, free southerners, and northerners.
ISBN 0–531–20252–6
1. United States—History—Civil War, 1861–1865—Participation, Afro-American—
    Juvenile literature.   2. Afro-American soldiers—History—19th century—
    Juvenile literature.   [1. United States—History—Civil War, 1861–1865—
    Participation, Afro-American.   2. Afro-American soldiers—History.
    3. Soldiers.]   I. Title.   II. Series.
E540.N3B58   1997
973.7'415—DC20

                                                                    96–31630
                                                                        CIP
                                                                         AC

CONTENTS

Chapter One
A White Man's War

Slavery in the North American colonies had its beginning in 1619 when twenty slaves were delivered to Jamestown, Virginia. During the next 250 years, as the colonies fought for freedom and the United States was formed, slavery became a part of the nation itself.

Landing slaves from Africa, at Jamestown in the Virginia Colony

By 1860, as war was about to start, the African-American population in the United States had grown to approximately 4,500,000. In the South, there were about four million slaves and 250,000 free African-Americans. In the North, there were about 225,000 free African-Americans.

Slavery was an awful thing. Not only did the southern white owner have complete physical control over his slaves, but he also had control of their spiritual and mental lives. Many owners viewed an intelligent or educated slave as dangerous. It was in the interest of the master to keep all of his slaves as ignorant as possible. Many owners also believed in keeping them afraid.

The 250,000 free African-Americans in the South did not live much better than the slaves. They had no civil rights and could not vote. They were almost completely segregated and had little chance for advancement. There were no public schools for them, and only a few free black people achieved any degree of education or business success. A few wealthy African-Americans, who were mostly very light-colored people of mixed race, even owned their own slaves.

The 225,000 free black people in the northern states

Before the Civil War, few free African-Americans could have become prosperous businessmen like this man, pictured with his wife in 1890.

Opposite: *A rally opposing the slave-catching rules ordered by the Fugitive Slave Law of 1850 was held in Milwaukee, Wisconsin, in 1854.*

were slightly better off. Most could attend public schools and form organizations that spoke out for their rights. In reality, though, they were still at the bottom of a segregated society. Prejudice against black people was strong. Schools in many of the northern states were segregated. Public transportation, hotels, and restaurants were also segregated in much of the North. Black people were definitely second-class citizens.

ANTI-SLAVE-CATCHERS'
MASS
CONVENTION!

All the People of this State, who are opposed to being made SLAVES or SLAVE-CATCHERS, and to having the Free Soil of Wisconsin made the hunting-ground for *Human Kidnappers*, and all who are willing to unite in a

 *STATE LEAGUE,*

to defend our State Sovereignty, our State Courts, and our State and National Constitutions, against the flagrant usurpations of U. S. Judges, Commissioners, and Marshals, and their Attorneys; and to maintain inviolate those great Constitutional Safeguards of Freedom—the WRIT OF HABEAS CORPUS, and the RIGHT OF TRIAL BY JURY—as old and sacred as Constitutional Liberty itself; and all who are willing to sustain the cause of those who are prosecuted, and to be prosecuted in Wisconsin, by the agents and executors of the Kidnapping Act of 1850, for the alleged crime of rescuing a human being from the hands of kidnappers, and restoring him to himself and to Freedom, are invited to meet at

YOUNGS' HALL,
IN THIS CITY,
THURSDAY, APRIL 13th,

At 11 o'clock A. M., to counsel together, and take such action as the exigencies of the times, and the cause of imperilled Liberty demand.

FREEMEN OF WISCONSIN! In the spirit of our Revolutionary Fathers, come up to this gathering of the Free, resolved to speak and act as men worthy of a Free Heritage. Let the plough stand still in the furrow, and the door of the workshop be closed, while you hasten to the rescue of your country. Let the Merchant forsake his Counting Room, the Lawyer his Brief, and the Minister of God his Study, and come up to discuss with us the broad principles of Liberty. Let Old Age throw aside its crutch, and Youth put on the strength of manhood, and the young men gird themselves anew for the conflict; and faith shall make us valiant in fight, and hope lead us onward to victory; "for they that be for us, are more than they that be against us." Come, then, one and all, from every town and village, come,

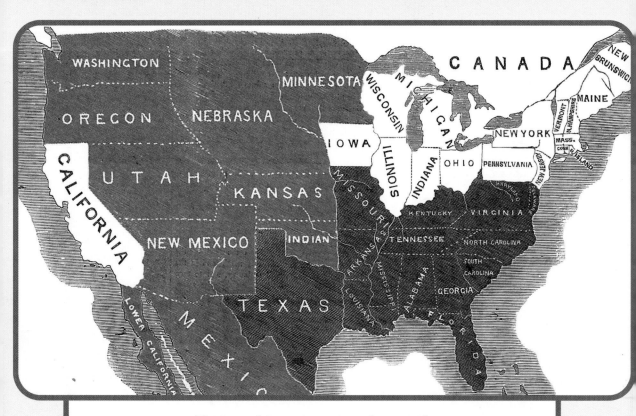

The United States as it existed in 1856.
Free states are shown in white and slave states in black.
The remainder was mostly unsettled territory.

The United States was the last of the major nations of the world to retain slavery. In the years from 1840 to 1860, sentiment against this evil was growing. Many white people came to believe that slavery should be abolished and that African-Americans should not face discrimination in their daily lives. Some Southerners also felt strongly against slavery, but few had the courage to speak out.

THE WAR BEGINS

Step by step, the United States Congress passed laws that made it more and more difficult for new states to allow slavery. In the South, where slavery was an institution, people grew angry at the idea that the federal government had more power than individual states. They believed they had the right to decide for themselves how they should live.

Finally, in 1861, eleven states—South Carolina, North Carolina, Georgia, Alabama, Florida, Texas, Virginia, Mississippi, Louisiana, Tennessee, and Arkansas—seceded, or withdrew, from the United States. They formed a new country, the Confederate States of America.

War was declared in April 1861, when Confederate forces in South Carolina attacked Fort Sumter in Charleston Harbor, forcing the federal troops there to surrender. President Abraham Lincoln immediately called up 70,000 men for service in the Union army. The newly formed Confederacy, confident that it had right and might on its side, called up 300,000.

Hundreds of African-Americans tried to enlist in the Union army right away, but they were turned down—a law passed in 1792 kept nonwhite people from fighting in the army. Most northern whites were ready to abolish slavery, but at the same time, they thought that black people were an inferior race, not fit to bear arms. They wanted to keep the rebellion of the southern states as a "white man's war."

Oddly enough, the recruitment of African-Americans into the United States Navy had never been outlawed. The navy took advantage of that fact by taking in many black men, though they mostly did heavy labor.

Abraham Lincoln was against slavery. But during the early months of the war, he was also against the recruitment of African-Americans. He was trying hard to keep the war as a battle against the idea of states having the right to secede instead of against the idea of slavery. Also, he was afraid that if the army took in black men, many prejudiced soldiers from the border states would throw down their arms and head south. Not until July of 1862 did Congress change the old law and allow the Union army to recruit free men "of African descent." For the next three years, African-Americans fought as hard as anyone.

Chapter Two

FREEDOM! THE EMANCIPATION PROCLAMATION

Many people, in the North and the South, both black and white, thought the United States could not be saved without overthrowing slavery. They thought that if the Union were preserved but slavery still existed in the South, the seventy-five-year-old nation would fall apart again.

Abolitionists—those who wanted to end slavery—argued that slaves were a source of strength to the Confederacy by the sheer fact of their numbers. The four million slaves in the South could farm and furnish labor for the Confederacy while white men fought.

FREDERICK DOUGLASS

The most important African-American abolitionist was an orator and editor by the name of Frederick Douglass. He had been a slave, but he escaped to the North. He educated himself and became a newspaper editor and speaker. After the fall of Fort Sumter in April 1861, Douglass wrote in his paper, *Douglass' Monthly:*

At last our proud Republic is overtaken. Our National Sin has found us out. . . . We have sown the wind, only to reap the whirlwind. . . . Could we write as with lightning, and speak as with the voice of thunder, we would write and should cry to the nation. REPENT, BREAK EVERY YOKE, LET THE OPPRESSED GO FREE, FOR HERE ON ALONE IS DELIVERANCE AND SAFETY. . . . Fire must be met with water, darkness with light, and war for the destruction of slavery. . . . This war with the slaveholders can never be brought to a desirable termination until slavery, the guilty cause of all our national troubles, has been totally and forever abolished.

THE LEGAL PROBLEM

As Union forces occupied border states and then invaded the Confederacy, slaves began to run away to Union camps. This had the effect of reducing the Confederate strength, but it left Lincoln with a problem.

The Fugitive Slave Law passed in 1850 stated that runaway slaves had to be returned to their masters. Most Union commanders followed the law and returned the runaway slaves to their southern homes. Frederick Douglass and others urged Lincoln to end the problem by proclaiming freedom for all slaves.

While the president was trying to decide what to do, Union General Benjamin F. Butler looked for another way to get around the Fugitive Slave Law. In May 1861, three slaves ran away from a Confederate labor battalion and escaped to the Union lines at Fort Monroe, Virginia. Butler, a former lawyer, called the slaves "contraband of war," meaning that they were enemy property and thus could be seized. He took them on as laborers for the Union army and refused to return them to their Confederate owners.

By the end of July, General Butler had more than a thousand contrabands. Other Union officers began to do

It was General Benjamin Butler who first called runaway slaves "contrabands" (meaning property of the enemy). These contrabands were some of the men Butler put to work as drivers.

the same thing. On August 6, the United States Congress passed a Confiscation Act, which allowed the North to seize all property, including slaves, used "in aid of the rebellion."

FRÉMONT ACTS ON HIS OWN

Union General John Charles Frémont, in command of the Western Division of War, with headquarters in St. Louis, Missouri, was a devout abolitionist. He had become a national hero for his journeys through the West. He did not agree with the policy of not permitting black men to fight in the war.

In Missouri, Frémont had to deal with a very divided population. It was a border state, where

Explorer and abolitionist General John C. Frémont was ahead of his time in wanting to allow blacks to fight for their own freedom.

southern sympathizers attacked those who believed in the Union. And sometimes Union supporters attacked the Southerners. No one was safe.

Hoping to calm the turmoil, Frémont declared martial law in the state in 1861. In what has been called the "first emancipation proclamation," he said that all persons engaged in activities against the government were guilty of treason. Under his order, the property of those people, including slaves, could be confiscated, or seized, by Union troops. The confiscated slaves were given their freedom.

As soon as news of Frémont's actions reached Washington, President Lincoln became fearful that border states would join the Confederacy. Lincoln canceled Frémont's order and removed him from his command. Only a few former slaves had received their freedom papers in the days before that happened.

Many Northerners welcomed Frémont's actions. The pressure was on for the president and Congress to find ways to free slaves in those border states that had remained loyal to the Union.

Taking the next step, on April 16, 1862, Congress freed the few thousand slaves living in the District of

Famous cartoonist Thomas Nast's celebration of Emancipation

Columbia by paying their owners for them, whether they wanted to sell or not. These freed slaves could now be paid normal wages and seek other gainful employment.

Congress then passed another bill to abolish slavery in the territories that had not yet been made states. A second Confiscation Act declared all slaves of Confederate masters "forever free" if they could reach Union lines.

LINCOLN WRESTLES WITH EMANCIPATION

Lincoln could no longer pretend that the war that had broken apart the nation had nothing to do with slavery. In the summer of 1862, he began to think seriously about freeing all slaves. His administration, however, felt that the North needed some major battlefield victories before they could issue a complete Emancipation Proclamation. It would be more successful if done from a position of strength.

Finally, following the Union victory at the Battle of Antietam on September 17, 1862, Lincoln issued a preliminary Emancipation Proclamation. It gave warning to the southern states that they must lay down their arms or their slaves would be freed. On January 1, 1863, President Lincoln kept his word. By virtue of his wartime powers and as commander in chief, the president proclaimed that all slaves in the rebellious southern states were "thence forward and forever free."

African-Americans and their supporters hailed the Emancipation Proclamation with joy. The Civil War had now become an even greater cause than preserving the Union.

Chapter Three

Turning Laborers into Soldiers

At the beginning of the war, neither the North nor the South was willing to arm African-Americans and make them full-fledged soldiers. Even though most

White Union army officers gave little thought at first to including freed African-Americans in their circles.

northern soldiers regarded slavery as an evil, they also believed that black men were not capable of fighting alongside whites or joining in the war effort.

Because the African-American population in the North was so limited, most Northerners had little experience dealing with black people, and they wished to keep it that way. They quickly found, however, that forming labor battalions of black volunteers freed many whites for active duty in the army.

Before slaves in Washington, D.C., gained their freedom, the quartermaster corps headquarters employed more than five hundred of them to do various menial tasks. Fighting regiments hired hundreds more as housekeepers, laundresses, and general laborers. Throughout the North, many free African-Americans were paid servants and workers.

In the South, slaves dug trenches, drove supply wagons, and did much of the dirty work that kept the Confederate war effort alive. Others accompanied their masters into battle. These slaves usually were not allowed to carry arms, though there were reports of slaves fighting to a limited extent as early as the Battle of Bull Run in August 1861.

A GIFT
TO THE UNION

In June 1861, William Tillman, a free African-American, was serving as cook and steward on a Union schooner, the *S. J. Waring*. The Union vessel was captured by a Confederate warship. A crew of seven Southerners boarded the *Waring* to sail it to a Confederate port. Tillman, left on board to fulfill his regular duties, was told that he would be sold as a slave when the ship arrived in Charleston.

That night, after the crew was asleep, Tillman took a heavy club and killed the captain and two others. He managed to subdue the other Southerners and place them in irons. Tillman sailed the *Waring* to New York, where he turned the ship over to the authorities. The *New York Times* noted that the nation was "indebted for the first vindication of its honor on the sea." The man who refused to be a slave was awarded a $6,000 prize and became one of the first heroes of the war.

*This Union camp welcomed a black contraband,
but only as the officers' servant.*

When General Butler treated runaway slaves as contraband of war and put them to work, thousands more slaves escaped and headed for Union camps. All along the battle lines, they were taken in and put into labor battalions. Perhaps what they found most exciting was the fact that they earned wages for their labor. More than a hundred thousand contraband men and women became available to the North during the next several years. But they still weren't soldiers.

REINFORCEMENTS

In May 1862, Union Army General David Hunter decided to form a regiment of ex-slaves living on the Sea Islands of South Carolina. They would be under the command of white officers. Many whites who lived there doubted that the men would make good soldiers. As one of the doubters said, "They are afraid, and they know it."

Hunter claimed he needed the men to reinforce his regular troops, which occupied the states of South Carolina, Florida, and Georgia. Washington wasn't yet ready to accept that step. Hunter later wrote that his regiment, which he called the 1st South Carolina Volunteers, was "a marvelous success."

Believe it or not, in the very southern city of New Orleans, the Confederates had enlisted free black men in state militia organizations. These men were willing to fight for the right to own slaves because they themselves were slave owners. They never actually left New Orleans to fight, though, and were still there when General Butler was sent from Virginia to occupy the city after its capture by the Union in April 1862. When the enthusiastic black regiment offered its services to Butler, he turned them down.

By August, however, Butler needed more soldiers. Without waiting for approval from the government, he reversed his decision, and within two weeks more than one thousand black troops were enlisted and formed into a regiment. They were initially called the *Corps d'Afrique,* but General Butler changed their name to the Louisiana Native Guards.

FACING THE FACTS

The Union army suffered a number of severe defeats at the hands of Confederate troops in the summer of 1862. Enlistment of white men dwindled as people became discouraged. On July 17, 1862, Congress, looking for an answer, finally approved the enlistment of black men into the army.

One of the first generals to take action was General Rufus Saxton, who took Hunter's place at Sea Islands, South Carolina. He formed five regiments, enlisting five thousand black men for military service and fifty thousand more as laborers.

The 1st South Carolina Volunteers lined up behind their white officers while training for battle in the South.

Under the command of Colonel Thomas Wentworth Higginson, a new 1st South Carolina Volunteers was formed. In his diary, which was later published as *Army Life in a Black Regiment*, Higginson wrote that he had

African-American riflemen waiting as the enemy approaches

"perfect confidence" in the former slaves' ability to be trained. He knew "that they had home and household and freedom to fight for." He was right. After only limited training, the ex-slaves went into battle in Florida and South Carolina. In these southern areas, they saw other black people still held in slavery.

THE MATTER OF PAY

As a sign of the prejudice which many Northerners felt against African-Americans, the first black soldiers enlisted in the Union army were to receive $10 a month, and the $3 cost of their uniforms was to be deducted from their pay. White soldiers received $13 a month plus the $3 fee for uniforms. Several people objected, but the U.S. Congress regarded the black men as laborers, not true soldiers.

The 54th Massachusetts Regiment was promised equal pay when it was formed in 1863 as the first regiment of free northern African-Americans. Even though the state's governor offered to make up the difference, the men refused to accept any pay until they were paid the same as white soldiers.

Not until March 1865 did Congress agree to match black pay to white pay, back to when the soldiers first enlisted. And even then, the black soldiers did not receive the money due them until after the war ended.

The encampment for the African-American soldiers in the Union's Army of the James River in Virginia

On October 28, 1862, African-American soldiers went into battle for the first time. The 79th United States Colored Infantry (called the lst Kansas Regiment in its first months of existence) fought Confederate forces at Island Mounds, Missouri. They had orders to clear an island in the Osage River of a force of about six hundred Southerners. The new black soldiers faced the enemy for the first time and successfully drove them from their position and into retreat.

FINDING WHITE OFFICERS

In late 1862, there were various efforts to organize African-Americans into armed regiments. Most of these regiments were commanded by white officers.

Not all white officers could be trusted to deal sympathetically with the black men in their commands. There seemed to be a built-in prejudice, even though most northern troops had never even had contact with African-Americans. It was easier, however, to become an officer of a black regiment than of a white regiment, so the opportunity appealed to many men.

The Bureau of Colored Troops was formed in May 1863, headed by Major Charles W. Foster. His role was to supervise and create local boards to recruit black soldiers and to select white officers to command them. Schools were formed to train the prospective officers, who had to have good recommendations from upstanding citizens. About one in four applicants was given a commission in the United States Colored Troops (USCT).

The examining boards were supposed to find those men who were morally fit and who cared about "uplifting" the black men under them. Some boards did a good job, and some did not. Many underqualified applicants slipped into the ranks of the white officer corps. Other excellent applicants were rejected. There were many tales of white officers taking advantage of African-Americans, such as taking their money or abusing them. But there were even more stories of respect that grew between the men of two different races.

During the final two years of the war, as many as 123,000 African-Americans at a time were in the uniform of the United States Colored Troops. The bureau helped a total of 186,000 black soldiers serve the country that was becoming truly their own.

Chapter Four

The 54th Massachusetts and More

On January 25, 1863, the War Department authorized Governor John Andrew of Massachusetts to raise companies of black volunteers for artillery and infantry. Mayor Stearns of Medford, Massachusetts, was appointed commissioner for the organization of the black troops. Volunteers were to serve for three years and were to receive the same pay as white enlisted men, which was $13.00 a month plus $3.00 for uniforms.

Governor Andrew asked Robert Gould Shaw to command these regiments. Shaw was then a captain with the 2nd Massachusetts Infantry. He had performed with valor in a number of battles with the Confederates. Even

Bostonian Captain Robert Gould Shaw accepted command of the 54th Massachusetts Regiment in 1863. A dedicated abolitionist, he was certain that African-Americans could be taught to fight as well as white men.

more important, he was known to believe that black men could fight. He was given a chance to prove that he was right.

Captain Shaw assumed command of the 54th Massachusetts Regiment. He was soon joined by nineteen other white officers, fourteen of whom had previously been on active duty.

RECRUITING SOLDIERS

Not very many African-Americans lived in Massachusetts, so recruiting drives took place in several different places in the North. Frederick Douglass, the famous black abolitionist, and other leaders helped recruit black soldiers to the Union effort. Douglass's son, Lewis, was among the first to volunteer.

In a call to arms to "men of color," Frederick Douglass said,

Liberty won by white men would lack half its lustre. Who would be free themselves must strike the blow. Better even to die free than to live slaves. . . . By every consideration which binds you to your enslaved fellow countrymen, and the peace and welfare of your country; by every aspiration which you cherish for the freedom and equality of yourselves and your children; by all the ties of blood and identity which make us one with the brave black men now fighting our battles in Louisiana, in South Carolina, I urge you to fly to arms, and smite with death the power that would bury the Government and your liberty in the same hopeless grave.

The banner beneath this recruiting poster read:
COME AND JOIN US BROTHERS.

Not only were there enough recruits for the 54th, but an extra thousand men formed an additional regiment, the 55th. All volunteers were sent to Camp Meigs near Boston, where they were provided with living quarters, uniforms, and arms.

On April 2, the 54th held its first dress parade, and the regiment was presented with flags the men would carry into battle. On May 28, they marched through Boston to the steamer *De Molay*. Their equipment and horses were taken aboard in the early afternoon. All the men boarded, too, and the ship set sail for Hilton Head, South Carolina, where General Hunter would lead them into combat.

The 54th Massachusetts was the first major unit enlisted and trained in the North and made up entirely of northern African-American men. These and the other black soldiers showed their heroism and courage while suffering great losses. Northerners who had questioned whether African-American troops could fight under pressure now saw them prove their worth.

THE 54TH AT FORT WAGNER

Charleston, South Carolina, was a prime target for the Union. The Civil War had begun at Fort Sumter in its harbor. After that, Confederate ships smuggled goods into the port at Charleston to supply the South. The sturdy forts guarding the entrance to the harbor were extremely well built for the defense of Charleston.

The 54th Massachusetts, newly arrived from Boston, went into battle on James Island on July 16, 1863. The

PROVING THEIR VALOR
ON THE MISSISSIPPI

The Battle of Port Hudson took place on May 27, 1863, near Baton Rouge, Louisiana. The 1st and 3rd Louisiana Negro Regiments stationed at Baton Rouge received orders to join Union troops at Port Hudson.

White Union troops had been attempting to take the Confederate-held fort for a week, but they were failing. Capturing Port Hudson would give the Union control of the Mississippi River from Port Hudson to Vicksburg, Mississippi. The black troops were ordered to attack the fort, which was occupied by more than six thousand Confederates.

The African-American soldiers had to attack at a point where the southern soldiers occupied a high bluff. They tried several times to charge across but were driven back. At one point they managed to drive the Confederate infantry from their rifle pits, or trenches. The new soldiers valiantly held those trenches for three hours before they were driven out by the determined Southerners.

Six hundred of the nine hundred African-Americans in the two regiments were killed, along with their two highest officers. Port Hudson was not taken until July, after it had been under siege for forty-seven days.

For months, General Ulysses S. Grant had besieged the city of Vicksburg in an effort to control the entire Mississippi River. Many slaves—often pursued by baying dogs—flocked to the "safety" of Grant's army. They formed African-American regiments, which, with only a few days of training, fought at Milliken's Bend, Louisiana, against 1,500 determined Confederates from Texas.

On the morning of June 7, 1863, the Confederates attacked. Learning that the men they were facing were former slaves, they advanced under the battle cry of "No quarter!" This meant "Don't show any mercy!" The two sides met on top of the levees, or raised riverbanks, in close, bloody combat with bayonets. The Confederates were forced to retreat from the earthworks. The African-American troops had proved their valor in the first large-scale battle to involve black soldiers.

Confederates outnumbered them, and they were driven back. Tired and bloody, they were ordered to attack Fort Wagner. This heavily fortified battery on the north end of Morris Island was about a mile and a half from Fort Sumter. It was the most important fort on the harbor, and it blocked the way to Charleston.

The 54th could get into position only by marching through mud and marshes for two days. The hungry and exhausted regiment arrived to find that they had been chosen to lead the attack on the fort.

Fort Wagner was surrounded on three sides by water, swamps, moats, and trenches. The only direct access was a narrow strip of dry ground. Led by the regiment's commander, Colonel Shaw, the 630 officers and men advanced across the narrow approach to the fort. As the charging troops came within range of Confederate guns, the guns fired, and men fell by the dozens. But those left standing did not retreat. They continued their charge, wading through a half-filled moat and up the parapets of the fort. There they came into hand-to-hand contact with the enemy.

At the height of the combat, Colonel Shaw fell, mortally wounded. The flag-bearer beside him also was shot.

The 54th Massachusetts storming Fort Wagner

The overall commander, General George Strong, who had vastly underestimated the strength of the Confederate battery, also died. Retreat was called, and those still able to move left the parapet and fled back across the access route. Bullets and bursting shells continued to take their toll. Forty percent of the brave men of the 54th were killed or wounded.

A memorial to Colonel Shaw and his heroic 54th Massachusetts Regiment of African-American soldiers stands in Boston.

In one sense, the battle at Fort Wagner resulted in a complete defeat of the 54th, especially because it took another seven weeks for the Union to capture the fort. But in another sense, the battle was a triumph for the soldiers. In the face of heavy odds, the heroic 54th showed the African-Americans' courage and willingness to die for a cause.

The regiment continued to fight skirmishes and battles throughout the South, under the command of Colonel E. N. Hollowell. They fought valiantly in the Battle of Olustee in Florida in February 1864 and returned to Boston to a heroes' welcome.

African-American troops participated in more than four hundred battles during the Civil War. The conduct of the men of the 54th Massachusetts Regiment was an example that inspired all Union soldiers, black and white.

The Congressional Medal of Honor

Chapter Five
ABOVE AND BEYOND

With all the action seen by so many African-American troops during the Civil War, there were many acts of heroism that will forever be unknown. Some actions, however, were singled out as being worthy of the highest American award for heroism and bravery in action—the Congressional Medal of Honor. The United States Congress created this medal in December 1861. It remains the nation's highest medal for "conspicuous gallantry . . . above and beyond the call of duty."

Medals of Honor were awarded to thirteen black men after action at Chaffin's Farm, near Richmond, Virginia. In this assault against a Confederate fortification, on September 29–30, 1864, black units lived up to their growing reputation for incredible bravery against impossible odds.

Wading through swamps right under the guns of the enemy, they were unable to reload, but they continued to move forward. In doing so, many of them died. One company commander later reported, "They fought splendidly that morning, facing the red tempest of death with unflinching heroism."

The thirteen recipients were:

William H. Barnes—though wounded, he was among the first to enter the Confederate fortifications.

Powhatan Beaty—when all his officers had been put out of action, this sergeant took command.

James H. Bronson—when all his officers had been put out of action, this sergeant led his company.

Nathan H. Edgerton—when three successive flag-bearers had been wounded and were unable to carry the flags, Edgerton, wounded himself, seized the flag and carried it into battle.

Christian A. Fleetwood—when his company's flag-bearers had been shot down, this college graduate took the colors and carried them throughout the battle.

James Gardiner—rushing in ahead of his brigade, he shot a Confederate officer and then ran him through with his bayonet.

A company of the 4th Colored Infantry,
photographed at the end of the war

Alfred B. Hilton—seizing his regimental and national flags from a fallen flag-bearer, this sergeant carried the colors until he himself was wounded.

Milton M. Holland—led his company after the officers had become casualties.

Miles James—even though one arm had been seriously wounded and he was within easy range of the enemy, he continued the fight, loading and firing his shoulder weapon with one hand. The mutilated arm was later amputated.

A HERO IS BORN
AT THE HELM OF A SHIP

Slave Robert Smalls had been hired out by his owner to a shipyard in Charleston, South Carolina, for ten years when the Civil War started. He had become a qualified sailor and pilot of a side-wheeler, the *Planter,* which was capable of carrying 1,400 bales of cotton. The Confederate Navy gave him missions to carry out in the coastal waters of South Carolina.

Smalls didn't want to help the South. He secretly notified the Union navy that he would be delivering a ship to them. On May 13, 1862, Smalls and his brother led several other slaves in taking control of the *Planter*. Dressed in the captain's uniform, Smalls performed all the proper signals that allowed his ship to move freely. He picked up his and his crews' families. By then it was daylight, but he sailed right past the guns of Fort Sumter and out to sea. Then he lowered the Confederate flag and turned the ship over to the Union.

The United States Navy not only acquired an additional ship—one badly needed by the Confederacy—but its armament and cargo as well. Smalls received his papers of freedom, was declared captain of the ship, and participated in at least seventeen engagements. He was a true American hero.

Alexander Kelly—in the face of great danger near the enemy lines, this first sergeant rescued his company's colors and raised them, rallying the men.

Robert Pinn—he took command of his company after all officers had been put out of action.

Edward Ratcliff—when his officers had been killed or wounded, he led the company right into the enemy's fortifications.

Charles Veal—Private Veal, seeing his company's flag-bearers shot by the enemy's lines, took the U.S. flag and carried it through the remainder of the battle.

OTHER ARMY ACTION

Five other African-American soldiers were awarded the Congressional Medal of Honor:

William H. Carney, 54th Massachusetts—fighting at Fort Wagner, South Carolina, he took the colors from a fallen flag-bearer and planted them on the Confederate parapet. When his company was forced to retreat, he retrieved the flag while being wounded twice.

Decatur Dorsey—he moved far ahead of his regiment at Petersburg, Virginia, and planted the colors on

An artist's view of the charge of the 22nd Negro Regiment at Petersburg, Virginia, in 1864

the Confederate works. Driven back, he continued to rally his colleagues.

William Appleton—also fighting at Petersburg, he was the first of his company to enter the enemy's lines. He inspired the troops during a desperate assault.

James H. Harris—at New Market Heights, Virginia, he was honored for "gallantry in the assault."

Thomas Hawkins—he rescued the regimental colors in the face of fierce fighting at Deep Bottom, Virginia.

NAVAL HEROES

During the Civil War, almost thirty thousand African-Americans served in the United States Navy, making up about one-fourth of all sailors. Many of them were escaped slaves, or contrabands, who were found to have skills that were needed by the navy. Many of them had experience sailing the rivers and harbors of the southern coasts as well as inland rivers and lakes. Unlike the soldiers, the black sailors were never given pay equal to the white sailors.

Naval records did not always note whether a sailor was black or white, but at least four naval Congressional Medal of Honor winners are recognized as being African-Americans:

Aaron Anderson—serving aboard the USS *Wyandunk* on March 18, 1865, Anderson bravely continued to fight as part of a boat crew even though devastating enemy fire shot away his oars, damaged his weapons, and blasted in the sides of his boat.

Robert Blake—this contraband, tending a cannon on the steam gunboat *Marblehead* on December 25, 1863, helped to drive the enemy from their position, forcing them to leave behind valuable weapons.

John Lawson—serving on the USS *Hartford* during successful attacks on Fort Morgan and various enemy vessels in the attack on Mobile Bay, he was seriously

Aboard the United States gunboat Mendota, *black and white sailors lived and worked together.*

wounded when an enemy shell exploded near his gun station. Lawson refused to go for medical treatment and continued to man his gun for the remainder of the action.

Joachim Pease—a seaman aboard the USS *Kearsarge* when it destroyed the Confederate ship *Alabama* near Cherbourg, France. Acting as a loader on the Number 2 gun, Pease remained cool in the face of devastating fire.

Confederate raider **Alabama** *sinking after an attack by the* **Kearsarge**

AFTER THE WAR . . .

In 1863, African-Americans had already been fighting long enough for the *Chicago Tribune* to observe: "Wherever a Negro has been tried, the courage, steadfastness, and endurance of the African race have been triumphantly vindicated. The Negro will fight for his liberty, for his place among men, for his right to develop himself in whatever direction he chooses; he will prove himself a hero, and if need be, a martyr."

It has been estimated that without the use of black troops by the Union, the Civil War would have continued for at least another year, with mounting loss of life on both sides. Black men earned reputations as valiant, trustworthy, and intelligent people.

A *New York Times* editorial written in 1866 noted: "It is evident from our experience that we can raise a large black army in this country: that the negroes are capable of being transformed into soldiers; that they can fight, and can do efficient work in all arms of service; that they have the sentiment of loyalty, and are capable of devotion to the flag."

The African-Americans' record in the Civil War was the main argument that people used when it was proposed that the United States Constitution be amended to give black males the right to vote. This Fifteenth Amendment was passed by Congress on February 26, 1869, and ratified by the states one year later. The men who had fought for their country would finally be given a share in the running of that country.

"THEIR TIME HAS FINALLY COME"

In September 1996, the African-Americans who served and died in the Civil War finally won recognition. As part of a week-long program, the African-American Civil War Memorial was dedicated.

The memorial is to be located in an inner-city park in the District of Columbia section called Shaw, named after Col. Robert Gould Shaw. A long, curving wall bears the names of 185,000 black soldiers and white officers. In front of it stands an 8-foot (2.4-m) bronze statue by Ed Hamilton of Louisville, Kentucky. The statue shows African-American soldiers and sailors who served, as well as the female family members they had to leave while they fought for their freedom.

Opposite: The statue for the African-American Civil War Memorial in Washington, D.C.

MAJOR EVENTS OF THE CIVIL WAR

1860
December 20   South Carolina is the first southern state to secede from the Union.

1861
February 4   Representatives from the seceding states meet in Montgomery, Alabama, and form the Confederate States of America.

February 18   Jefferson Davis, previously U.S. Secretary of War, is inaugurated as president of the Confederate States.

April 12   War begins at 4:30 A.M.. by a Confederate attack on Union-held Fort Sumter in South Carolina.

April 15   President Abraham Lincoln calls for 75,000 volunteers to help stop the war with the Confederacy.

April 19   Lincoln orders a naval blockade of southern seaports.

July 21   The First Battle of Bull Run (or Manassas) in Virginia is the first important battle; it is won by Confederate troops.

August 10   The Battle of Wilson's Creek in Missouri, another Confederate victory, brings lands west of the Mississippi into the war.

1862
February 16   The fall of Fort Donelson in Tennessee to General Ulysses S. Grant's Union troops opens up Nashville to capture; Nashville becomes the first southern city to be taken by the North.

March 9   The first battle of ironclad ships, the *Monitor* and the *Merrimack* (called the *Virginia* by the Confederacy), ends in a draw but revolutionizes naval warfare.

April 25   New Orleans, Louisiana, is captured by a fleet under the command of David Farragut.

September 4   General Robert E. Lee's Confederate troops move into Maryland, invading the North for the first time and heading toward Pennsylvania.

September 17   Lee's advance is stopped by the Battle of Antietam (or Sharpsburg) in Maryland, in the war's bloodiest day of fighting.

1863
January 1   The Emancipation Proclamation is signed, granting freedom to all slaves within the seceded states.

March 3   The U.S. Congress approves the conscription, or draft, of all able-bodied males between the ages of 20 and 45.

May   The first all–African-American regiment in the Union army, the 54th Massachusetts, begins serving.

June 3	Lee begins another advance into the North.
June 9	The Battle of Brandy Station in Virginia turns into the largest cavalry action of the war; the North is forced to retreat.
July 1–3	The Battle of Gettysburg in Pennsylvania ends Lee's attempt to take the North. From this time on, the Confederates fight a defensive battle within their own states.
July 3	The siege of Vicksburg, Mississippi, ends in a Union victory.
July 8	Port Hudson, Louisiana, surrenders, effectively cutting the Confederacy in half as the Union takes control of the entire Mississippi River.
July 13–16	Riots in New York City protesting the draft kill or injure hundreds.
November 19	President Lincoln delivers the Gettysburg Address as a dedication of the new national cemetery at Gettysburg, Pennsylvania.

1864

March 10	General Grant is put in charge of the entire U.S. Army.
August 5	The Battle of Mobile Bay in Alabama is won by the Union fleet under Admiral Farragut.
September 1	The Union army, under General William T. Sherman, captures Atlanta, Georgia.
October 19	After more than two months of fighting in the Shenandoah Valley of Virginia, General Philip Sheridan's cavalry regiments take the valley in the Battle of Cedar Creek, leaving the Confederates without an important source of food or a place to regroup.
November	General Sherman's army marches the 300 miles (483 km) from Atlanta to the Atlantic Ocean, living off the land and destroying everything the Confederates might find useful.

1865

March 13	Out of desperation, the Confederate Congress votes to recruit African-American soldiers. Five days later, the Confederate Congress no longer exists.
April 2	Richmond, Virginia, the capital of the Confederacy, falls to the Union.
April 9	Lee surrenders to Grant at Appomatox Court House in Virginia.
April 14	Abraham Lincoln is shot by southern sympathizer John Wilkes Booth. He dies the next day.
December 18	The Thirteenth Amendment to the Constitution, abolishing slavery, goes into effect.

FOR MORE INFORMATION

FOR FURTHER READING

Hakim, Joy. *War, Terrible War.* A History of US, Book Six. New York:
    Oxford University Press, 1994.

Durwood, Thomas A., et al. *The History of the Civil War.* 10 vols. New
    York: Silver Burdett, 1990.

Tracey, Patrick. *Military Leaders of the Civil War.* American Profiles series.
    New York: Facts on File, 1993.

VIDEOS

The Civil War. 9 vols. Produced by Ken Burns. PBS Home Video.
The Civil War. 2 vols. Pied Piper.

CD-ROMS

African-American History—Slavery to Civil Rights. Queue.
American Heritage Civil War CD. Simon & Schuster Interactive.
Civil War: Two Views CD. Clearvue.
Civil War—America's Epic Struggle. 2 CD set. Multi-Educator.

INTERNET SITES

Due to the changeable nature of the Internet, sites appear and disappear very quickly. The resources listed below offered useful information on the Civil War at the time of publication. Internet addresses must be entered with capital and lowercase letters exactly as they appear.

The Yahoo directory of the World Wide Web is an excellent place to find Internet sites on any topic. The directory is located at:
http://www.yahoo.com

The Internet has hundreds of sites with information about the Civil War. The United States Civil War Center at Louisiana State University maintains a Web site for the gathering and sharing of information: ***http://www.cwc.lsu.edu***

The Civil War in Miniature by R. L. Curry is a collection of documented facts and interesting tidbits that brings many of the different facets of the Civil War together: ***http://serve.aeneas.net/ais/civwamin/***

The National Park Service maintains sites on hundreds of Civil War battles. The directory of these sites is at: ***http://www.cv.nps.gov/abpp/battles/camp.html***

INDEX

About the Author

Wallace B. Black was a pilot flying in India and China during World War II. Having lived history, he became fascinated by it. He is the author of a twenty-book series for young people about World War II. Building on his lifelong interest in the American Civil War and the West, he and his wife, Jean F. Blashfield, developed the American Civil War series for Franklin Watts, but he was able to write only two of the books before being sidelined by ill health.

Mr. Black graduated from the University of Illinois, played the saxophone in various wartime jazz bands, and worked in children's publishing all his life. He was the creator of many books and encyclopedias now found in schools and libraries.